CW00392721

SIKHISM

Roger Butler

Inspector for Religious Education
with the London Borough of Ealing

SERIES EDITOR: CLIVE ERRICKER

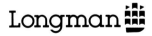

About the Themes in Religion series

This series of books offers a lively and accessible introduction to the six main world religions for students taking GCSE Religious Studies. The books can be used separately to study one religious tradition, or they can be used together, to investigate one theme across the traditions, such as beliefs, worship, pilgrimage or values. The section on values shows how each religion reacts to everyday life and the modern world. The spreads offer class activities and assignments that relate to coursework requirements and encourage further research, and each book provides a glossary of important terms and a reading list.

Each spread is self-contained and presents an important aspect of each religion. Through carefully chosen photographs, clear text and relevant quotations from scriptures and believers, students will learn about each religion and the living impact it has for believers today. The wide variety of assignments help pupils to evaluate what they have read, suggest activities to further their understanding, and raise issues for them to reflect on.

We hope that these books will provide students of all abilities with a stimulating introduction to these religions, and that the enjoyment of using them matches that of producing them.

Clive Erricker

About Sikhism

The Sikh religion has much to commend it for study at GCSE level. While it undoubtedly has teachings of great profundity and complexity, its central teachings are easily stated and understood. Its history is entirely contained within the last 500 years and there are significant Sikh communities in many of Britain's larger cities. Sikhs generally welcome interest being shown in their religion, and it is my hope that students will not only attain a qualification but also a degree of emapthy with and understanding of this vibrant and hardworking community. I also hope that some will find sufficent food for thought in the Sikh teachings that their own pattern of belief and behaviour will evolve as a result of their study and reflection.

Roger Butler

Thank You

Particular thanks are due to Balwant Singh Grewal of the British Sikh Education Council, Lou Singh Khalsa Angrez, Dr Chanan Singh Syan and Harbaksh Kaur Phull, each of whom read through the manuscript and pointed out errors and improvements. Others who helped me generously with their time included Tripatjit Kaur Bhamra, Satpal Kaur Jandu, Tarnjit Kaur, Biant Singh, Sakwinder Kaur, Janak Singh JP, Gurmail Singh Kandola, Daljit Singh, Bhupinder Singh, Parmjit Singh, Hindpal Singh, Maninder Singh Khalsa, Iqbal Singh, Anandia Lachmansingh and Baljeet Singh Samra. Three organisations which helped me greatly were the New Approach Mission for Occidental Sikhism, Nottingham's Sikh Community and Youth Service, and the Khalsa Centre in Tooting.

CONTENTS

WORSHIP

A VISIT TO A GURU-DWARA

A good way to begin our study of the **Sikh** religion is to go on a visit to a Sikh place of worship – a **Guru-dwara** (more easily said and therefore usually written as 'Gurdwara'). Guru-dwara literally means the 'Guru's door' through which one must go to meet the Guru. Sometimes Guru-dwaras are big and beautiful buildings that have been specially built. Often though, especially in places where Sikhs have only recently come to live, the Guru-dwara is more likely to have once been something else, like a church, a house or even a room in a flat. Let us visit one in South London on a Sunday morning. (There is nothing special about Sundays for Sikhs but in Britain it is the most convenient time for many people to get to a Guru-dwara.)

The Nishan Sahib

Outside the Guru-dwara there is a yellow triangular flag at the top of a pole which is covered with a cloth. Sikhs refer to this flag as **Nishan Sahib**. On the flag there are two curved swords (kirpans), a double-edged sword (**khanda**) and a circle (**chakkar**). This symbol is often simply referred to as the 'khanda'. (You can see the symbol on the banners in the picture.) As Sikhs enter the Guru-dwara they stop for a moment and pay their respects to the Nishan Sahib by either bowing to it or touching the base of the flag-pole.

A Guru-dwara in East Africa. Study this picture very carefully and make a list of everything you can see in it that you think might have particular significance for Sikhs

Inside the Guru-dwara

We enter this particular Guru-dwara through a side door into a small hall used for social functions and classes. Next we come to a kitchen where people are busily at work. Before we go further, into the most important room, we must take off our shoes and cover our heads.

We walk into the main hall of the Guru-dwara where there is a carpet on the floor. Straight ahead and facing us there is a man sitting cross-legged behind a large book which is resting on some cushions. He is reading aloud and occasionally waving his **chauri** (a sort of fan) over it as a mark of respect. The book, the Guru Granth Sahib, is to Sikhs much more than just a book (see pages 26–7). There are already about a hundred and fifty people sitting on the floor of the Guru-dwara – there are no chairs. Women are sitting on the left as we face the front, men on the right.

ASSIGNMENTS

● Before you continue reading this book take a large piece of paper and write the word 'Sikhs' in the middle. Around it write anything you already know about the Sikh religion. Then use a different colour pen to jot down any questions you would like answered by this book. As you read successive chapters add to your notes and cross off your questions as they are answered.

KEY WORDS

Sikh   Guru-dwara   Nishan Sahib
khanda   chakkar   chauri

WORSHIP IN THE GURU-DWARA

When Sikhs enter the main hall of a Guru-dwara they first walk straight to the front and kneel before the Guru Granth Sahib. With their hands and knees on the floor they bow down so that their heads touch the ground. They then may leave a gift which might be money, food or flowers. Perhaps next time we come we might like to pay our respects to the Sikhs' Guru in this way.

On the walls of the main hall of the Guru-dwara there are pictures of the ten Gurus, the great prophets of the Sikh religion. Other pictures show famous events in the history of the Sikhs. There are also pictures of beautiful Guru-dwaras in other parts of the world – particularly of the Harimandir Sahib (known by non-Sikhs as the Golden Temple) in Amritsar in the Indian state of Punjab. Some Sikhs believe strongly that there should not be pictures on the walls of Guru-dwaras as they can distract worshippers from remembering the presence of God. Other Sikhs say that so long as the pictures are on the back and side walls, so that they are not in view when one is worshipping, then there is no harm in them.

● Jews, Muslims and some Christians also believe that it is unacceptable to have images of living beings in a place devoted to the worship of God. What danger do you think believers might see in such decorations?

The morning worship lasts about two hours. It consists mainly of people chanting verses from the Guru Granth Sahib. Musicians known as **ragees** will sing and provide a musical accompaniment. Sometimes ragees are professional musicians, more often members of the congregation will take this role. Traditional instruments used are the **baja** and **tabla**, although Hindpal Singh, a young Sikh from Bedford, explained: 'There are now Guru-dwaras where Sikhs use guitars and other instruments to accompany workship.'

Towards the end of the time of worship there will always be a prayer said which the entire congregation will join in with, standing up and holding their hands together in front of them. This is called the **Ardas**.

The Adras is in fact more than a prayer. It begins with a recounting of the improtant facts of Sikh history; it then goes on to be a prayer for the Sikh community and all humankind, with a special mention for the local community. Here are a few lines from Ardas:

> O true King and loving Father, we have sung your sweet hymns, heard your word which gives life and talked of your many blessings. May these find a place in our hearts so that our souls may be drawn towards you.
> ... may the glory of your Name increase and may the whole world be blessed by your grace.

ਘਰੇ। ੴ ੳ ਗੁਰੁ ਗੋਬਿੰਦ ਹੁਇ ਪ੍ਰਗਟਿਆ ਦਸਵੇ ਅਵਤਾਰ। ਜਿਨ ਅ

Worship in a Guru-dwara in Canada

Finally, some food from a metal bowl is distributed to all those who are present. It is first blessed by being touched with a kirpan. Some Sikhs then bring it round in smaller bowls to all members of the congregation, no matter whether they are Sikhs or not. Sikhs would like you to accept this warm, moist, sweet piece of **karah parshad** that is put into your hand – you will understand why when you have read the next section.

Hindpal Singh looks forward to attending worship in the Guru-dwara, 'because it is a tremendous privilege to be in the presence of our Guru and to benefit from the company of the **sangat**.' ('Sangat' means 'congregation', the people gathered to worship.)

ASSIGNMENTS

● How do you think that going to a Guru-dwara would help a young Sikh child learn about her or his religion? Write down all the features of a Guru-dwara that would be helpful, with a brief explanation of the importance of each one.

● The photograph shows people performing a number of acts of devotion that have already been explained. What are they?

KEY WORDS

ragee   baja   tabla   Ardas
karah parshad   sangat

FOOD AND WORSHIP

The Sikh religion – **Sikhi** – started in the Punjab, in India, about five hundred years ago. Most people there were Hindu (some were Muslim). In the Hindu religion people are born into different 'castes' which used to determine things like what jobs they would do, what foods they could eat and with whom. Guru Nanak, the founder of the Sikh community (or **panth**), said that all people should be treated equally as children of the one God. By eating food together from the same bowl in the act of worship, Sikhs are demonstrating this belief. This is why karah parshad is always shared at any Sikh religious ceremony.

Langar

The langar

After the service is over, Sikhs (and anyone else present) will have the opportunity to share in a meal that has been prepared. A portion of this food will have been brought into the Guru-dwara before Ardas was said and will have been blessed by the Guru Granth Sahib. This blessed food is then mixed with the rest of the food that has been prepared. The meal, the place in which it is prepared and the place where it is eaten are all known as **langar** (or more properly as Guru-ka-langar). The langar might be held in a hall, outside in the courtyard or even in the main hall of the Guru-dwara once a curtain has been drawn to separate the Guru Granth Sahib from this activity. This meal is a chance for members of the sangat to get together, be sociable and to catch up on news about each other's families. But again there is this aspect of sharing food together and being prepared to eat with anyone. People sit in rows with no privileged positions, everyone eating the same food. This eating together in rows is known as **pangat**. It is not necessary to attend worship to eat food offered as langar at a Guru-dwara. Baljit Singh, a Sikh who lives in Nottingham, put it like this:

'Travellers, the poor, indeed anyone who wants to can turn up at a Guru-dwara to be fed. The food will be prepared and paid for by a family, or occasionally by the Guru-dwara management committee out of donations offered by the sangat.'

The food offered in a Guru-dwara will always be vegetarian. Not all Sikhs are vegetarian although many are. It is of course the case that a large number of people can be fed more cheaply when only vegetarian food is being used but Baljit Singh pointed out:

'There are two things to remember about Sikhs and food, firstly all the amrit-dhari Sikhs I know [see page 41] believe it is wrong to use living animals, which have a soul like us, as food, but secondly our Gurus taught us that we must eat only to sustain our bodies not for the pleasure of eating things that taste good.'

ASSIGNMENTS

● For what reasons do you think someone might offer to provide and prepare food for langar? Imagine you are asked to interview one of the people who is serving food in the photograph. Write a list of questions and that person's replies.

● Using your interview as a basis, write a short magazine article on langar. Include in your article why it is a religiously important part of Sikh community life. (You may wish to do some further research for this.)

KEY WORDS

Sikhi   panth   langar   pangat

DEVOTION TO GOD

Music in the Guru-dwara

Music is important in the Sikh religion. The Sikh holy book, the Guru Granth Sahib, is basically a collection of poems in praise of God set to music. These hymns are known as **shabad**, and the practice of singing hymns is known as **keertan**.

The hymns found in the Guru Granth Sahib are also known as **Gurbani**, 'the words of the Guru', and reading them with devotion and understanding is something Sikhs will try to do frequently. Dr Chanan Singh Syan explained:

'The writings of the Guru Granth Sahib are the words of God. The Guru Granth Sahib is filled with the same jot [light or spirit] as was in the human Gurus.'

The important thing is for Sikhs not simply to remember these words but to understand them and absorb them into their hearts. For most people it is far easier to remember songs than to commit poems or prose to memory. So music helps the Gurbani enter the believers' hearts.

● Think back to some songs you learned in primary school. Sing them now, in your head if you are in class, and think how many years it is since you last heard or sang them. Discuss what a powerful aid to memory music can be.

Nam simaran

Nam simaran literally means 'remembering God's name'. It has been said that all of the Sikh religion is bhakti (devotion to God) and that there are two aspects to bhakti: Nam simaran and sewa (see pages 52–3). The idea of Nam simaran is to grow ever closer to God by being constantly aware of his presence with you. The most usual way Sikhs try to remember God's presence is through **Nam japna**, which is the constant repetition, aloud or silently, of God's name 'Wahe-Guru' (wonderful lord/teacher).

All-night keertan

Some Sikhs belong to a group known as the Akand-Keertani Jatha and follow the teachings of a twentieth-century **mahapurkh** (holy person), Bhai Randir Singh. Among this group there is a practice known as 'ranus sebay', which involves gathering in a Guru-dwara to spend the whole night in keertan with everyone joining in the singing. Tarnjit Kaur, a physics student in London, is enthusiastic about it:

'The singing can be loud, but most importantly it is done with great devotion. Once I was at a ranus sebay in a Guru-dwara on the top of a hill and you could see the sun coming up as we sang the morning hymns. It was beautiful and it is amazing how after many hours of praising Wahe-Guru and drawing close to him no one feels tired.'

Musicians accompany keertan

ASSIGNMENTS

● What kind of thoughts fill your head during an average day? If you could change your thoughts would it change the sort of person you are? How might thinking constantly of God affect someone?

KEY WORDS

shabad   keertan   Gurbani
Nam simaran   Nam japna   mahapurkh

THE HARIMANDIR SAHIB

You may remember that on the walls of the Guru-dwara we visited there were pictures of the **Harimandir Sahib** in Amritsar. Harimandir means 'God's House', and Sahib is a word added to the names of some people, places and things to show how much they are respected. The Harimandir Sahib is the building which is often referred to by non-Sikhs as the 'Golden Temple'. This beautiful building has unhappily been much in the news in recent years because of a series of conflicts between some Sikh groups and the Indian authorities. So what exactly is the Harimandir Sahib, and what is its importance to Sikhs? The Harimandir

The Harimandir Sahib in Amritsar

Sahib is a Guru-dwara, but a very special Guru-dwara.

The fourth Guru of the Sikhs, Guru Ram Das, chose the place where the city of Amritsar is today on some land which was offered to the Sikhs by the Emperor Akbar. (Another tradition says that the Sikh community bought the land.) Guru Ram Das described the location as:

> a most sacred place, behold its beauty. This, truly, may be a gateway to deliverance.

At this place the Guru said a huge rectangular pool should be dug and filled with **amrit** (blessed water). Such a pool for bathing in is known as a 'serovar'. Ram Das's son, Guru Arjan, completed the work and in the middle of the serovar, on an island, had the Harimandir built. It was completed in 1601.

The Harimandir Sahib is a place that is very dear to all Sikhs. It might seem surprising that this Guru-dwara should have been a centre for so much conflict in recent years but this really is nothing new as you can see in this quotation:

> The [Harimandir Sahib] has had a chequered history in line with that of the Sikh community. It has always been a major rallying point for the Sikhs, and, when they were facing severe persecution... the [Harimandir Sahib] was captured by the Mughal rulers. It was desecrated and even razed to the ground and the holy tank filled up with filth... Around 1740 ... the ruler of Amritsar used the temple as a dancing hall, defiled the sacred precincts by employing the premises for drinking bouts and debauchery and barred all entry to the worshippers.

Sikhs who no longer live in the Punjab like to visit the Harimandir Sahib and other famous places associated with the lives of the Gurus and the history of the Sikh religion. Such a visit is known as a **yatra**. However, strictly speaking, Sikhs do not believe in pilgrimage in the way Hindus do. As God is everywhere for the Sikh, so no place on earth (or in the universe) can be more holy than any other place. Sikhs have a similar view of time and will never consult an astrologer about auspicious dates for weddings, journeys or anything else, as this would suggest that there were powers in the universe other than God.

ASSIGNMENTS

● Using the photograph, and what you have learned about the Harimandir Sahib, write a radio talk that would help listeners to imagine what it is like to be there.

● Look again at the way Guru Ram Das described the land on which the Harimandir Sahib came to be built, and then compare it with what was said above about pilgrimage. Is there a contradiction here? Discuss the matter and note your conclusions.

KEY WORDS

Harimandir Sahib   amrit   yatra

WORSHIP IN EVERYDAY LIFE

When devout Sikhs live near to a Guru-dwara they generally go there every morning to attend morning keertan and again in the evening to attend the evening keertan. However, where such daily attendance at a Guru-dwara is not possible, morning and evening prayers are normally said at home.

Getting up early

Guru Ram Das said, 'One who calls himself a Sikh gets up early.' Sikhs have a special word for the early morning – **amritvela**, and it is thought to be a good time for prayer and meditation.

Balwant Singh Grewal, who lives in London, told me about his mornings:

'On awakening, and before prayer, I take a bath. Having covered my head I say the morning prayers. First **Japji Sahib**, a hymn of Guru Nanak's, then there are other morning prayers to say, some by Guru Gobind Singh. Before the final prayer I have a period of meditation for perhaps 10 to 15 minutes. The entire cycle of morning prayers can take as long as two hours or even longer but on work days I normally spend only about an hour in prayer. It is not essential that one says them without a break or without doing other things.

There are no set positions for prayer. Often I make a cup of tea for other members of my family and wake them between saying Japji Sahib and the other prayers and if there is a real hurry then prayers can be said while making breakfast or doing other work provided that this work can be done without conscious attention. However, the ideal is to say one's prayers sitting down and undistracted.

It might appear disrespectful and distracting to pray while doing other things but in the Guru Granth Sahib (pages 1375–6) we read that when a great Hindu holy man, Trilochan, criticised his disciple Nam Dev for spending too long at his tailoring work, Nam Dev replied: "O Trilochan, speak your Lord's name with your mouth ‖ With your hand and your feet you may work."'

During the day, Sikhs practise Nam simaran by chanting, perhaps under their breath, **Wahe-Guru**, which they may intersperse with another of God's names – **Sat-Nam** (true name). One Sikh said she often finds herself walking along the road 'having a chit-chat with Wahe-Guru'.

After work there are evening hymns which are said before eating – **So-dar Rahiras**. Then before going to bed the devout Sikh will say the short selection of hymns known as Keertan Sohila.

God is remembered and his presence invoked in the daily order of prayer

True prayer

Devout Sikhs have a rich prayer life but
they will try never to forget the words
Guru Nanak directed at a Muslim who
had to pray five times daily:

> You offer five prayers, five times a day,
>   giving them different names.
> But let truth be your first prayer;
> Honest living the second;
> Invocation of His mercy for all, the
>   third;
> Honesty of mind, the fourth, and
> Fifth, the praise of the Lord.
> Let good deeds be your prayer.

ASSIGNMENTS

- In a sentence sum up what Guru Nanak was saying about
  the connection between prayer and the way a Sikh should
  live.

- Imagine you are a reporter on a local newspaper sent to
  cover the opening of a new Guru-dwara. You have spent a
  day there, attended worship, eaten a meal and talked to a
  number of Sikhs. Write a sympathetic article describing and
  explaining what you have seen and heard. Finish the article
  describing your own thoughts and feelings about the Sikh
  community.

KEY WORDS

| amritvela | Japji Sahib | Wahe-Guru |
| Sat-Nam | So-dar Rahiras | |

BELIEFS

GOD

The most important belief in the Sikh religion is that there is only one God. Sikhs believe that God is present everywhere and that people can learn to know and love God.

It has always been difficult for believers in God to explain to others what they believe God to be like but the Sikh religion sets out what it believes about God in the

Mool Mantra (a mantra is a prayer, sometimes a single word, which is repeated over and over again). The Mool Mantra is the first thing written in the Guru Granth Sahib and its first words, **ik onkaar** – 'there is only one God' – are written up on the walls of Guru-dwaras, worn on badges and used as a symbol, as in the photograph. If you look closely at these words in the

Gurmukhi script below or in the photograph, you will notice that the character which represents the word 'onkaar' has a bottom section, a middle section and a top section and then a line heading off to infinity. This character reminds Sikhs that God is all-encompassing and infinite.

IK ONKAAR
There is one and only one God
SAT NAAM
Truth is His Name
KARTA PURKH
He is the Creator
NIR BHAU
He is without fear
NIR VAIR
He is without hate
AKAAL MOORAT
Immortal/without form
AJOONI
He is beyond birth and death
SAIBHANG
He is self-illuminated (the Enlightener)
GUR PARSAAD
He is realised by the kindness of the true Guru

What is God like?

Notice that the second statement of the Mool Mantra tells us that God is Truth, Sat Naam. **Sat-Guru** (true teacher) is a common Sikh name for God.

You will have observed that the Mool Mantra seems to assume that God is male. God is normally regarded by Sikhs as masculine, with all Sikhs – men and women – being regarded as female in relation to God. The Guru Granth Sahib uses romantic images of a woman pining for her loved one as a metaphor for the way in which Sikhs desire God.

ASSIGNMENTS

● With a partner discuss how using both male and female pronouns for God might change a believer's feelings about God. Write up your conclusions.

● Copy the first line of the Mool Mantra – ik onkaar – in Gurmukhi into your book or folder. Do it large and coloured and try to commit the shape and sound to memory. Underneath write about the experience of doing this task, was it peaceful or irritating, easy or hard, as you expected or different? While you do this try not to talk or be distracted in any way.

KEY WORDS

Mool Mantra   ik onkaar   Sat-Guru

GURU

We have already learned that God is known by Sikhs as Wahe-Guru (wonderful Lord) or as Sat-Guru (true teacher). The Sikh religion had ten human Gurus, its holy book is the Guru Granth Sahib and its place of worship is a Guru-dwara (the Guru's gate or door). The Sikh community is known as the **Guru panth**. You will have realised by now that this word Guru and the idea behind it are very important in the Sikh religion.

What does Guru mean?

Dictionaries will usually tell you simply that a guru is a Hindu or Sikh religious teacher. Sikhs themselves understand that *Gu* means darkness and *Ru* means light so that a Guru leads people from darkness (a symbol of ignorance and falsehood) to light (a symbol of spiritual knowledge and truth).

As God, in Sikh belief, is all-knowing and all-wise, God is the perfect Guru. But Sikhs believe that God has become known by some very holy people who have been able to become at one with God in this life. The Sikh Gurus were such people, God's **jot** was in them. The holy book is Guru because the writings in it were inspired by God and are now the primary channel of God's communication with Sikhs. The Sikh community also came to believe that when representatives of the entire panth met together in the presence of the Guru Granth Sahib to discuss matters of importance then the intention of the Guru (the **Gurumata**) would become known, so the panth itself is Guru.

The definition of a Sikh

Daljit Singh, a Sikh who lives in Nottingham and who works as a personnel officer, explained what a Sikh is in these words:

> 'A Sikh is that person who believes in the ten Gurus, the continuing jot and the continuing guruship of the Guru Granth Sahib.'

The word 'jot' is an abbreviation for Rab(i) Jot – 'God's light, or God's spirit'. Daljit went on to explain the word 'jot' like this:

> 'It's not God but it's part of God. It's like rays of the sun. You can't call the sun's rays the sun, they're part of the sun. Or when a wave hits a rock and you get droplets of water spray up. The droplets are not the ocean but they are from the ocean. Jot emanates from the Divine Being but it is not the totality of that Being.'

ASSIGNMENTS

● You will see that the word 'Guru' is sometimes translated as 'teacher'. But someone once wrote an autobiography entitled 'Many Teachers but no Guru'. What might the writer have meant by that title?

● What qualities do you think it would have been important for a Sikh Guru to have had? Discuss this with a partner then write a list of five, explaining your reasons for each one. Now using the books on page 64 or others, write about two of the ten Sikh Gurus and explain the ways in which their qualities are similar to or different from those in your list.

KEY WORDS

Guru Panth   jot   Gurumata

Southampton Sikhs gather at Baisakhi

THE YOUNG GURU NANAK

Although Sikhs believe that God's jot was in all ten human Gurus and that they all carried the same message, we need to pay special attention to Guru Nanak, the first Guru and founder of the Sikh panth.

However, learning about the life of Guru Nanak is much more difficult than it sounds. Where are we to look for accurate information? There are many books that have been written about him but they are all based on some writings known as 'janam sakhis' (birth narratives) which were written many years after his death by people who were devoted to the Guru and his memory. The janam sakhis contain much material that appears to be legendary and they do not agree on certain details. What we are about to learn then is what Sikhs believe about Guru Nanak.

Guru Nanak's childhood

He was a child of smiles. Whoever saw him, or touched him accidentally, praised God. He was so beautiful, so mysteriously fair in colour and form with a radiance that was new to earth. He cast a spell that none could escape.

Guru Nanak was born in the area of India known as the Punjab (or Panjab). The Punjab is now partly in north-west India and partly in Pakistan. Guru Nanak's birthplace was a village called Talwandi which is now in Pakistan and renamed Nankana Sahib. When Nanak was growing up most of the people he met were either Hindu or Muslim. He quickly recognised that while both religions taught people to live a good, honest and holy life many of the followers of these religions did not live up to these teachings.

A disappointing son

As a child and a young man Nanak was a great disappointment to his father who had hoped that Nanak would grow up to be a successful businessman. But Nanak showed no interest in business matters. He went to three different schools and in each he showed great ability. He learned the Arabic and Persian languages easily and wrote beautiful poetry even when he was very young. The only subject he could not apply himself to was accounting and this was the subject his father most wanted him to be good at so that he could have a successful career. Here is a famous story about Guru Nanak's childhood:

He was once looking after some cows but became so lost in his own thoughts that he did not notice the cows straying into the next field where they trampled

Sikhs pray at the Guru Nanak Guru-dwara in the town where he was born, now called Nankana Sahib

and ate its crops. The farmer who owned the field was furious and had Nanak dragged before the headman of the village, Rai Bular, where Nanak was accused of being responsible for the damage caused. Nanak smiled and said: 'Go and see – there is no damage caused to the field.' When Rai Bular went to inspect the field for himself he found that Nanak was right, the field had been miraculously restored to its original state.

ASSIGNMENTS

● What does a Sikh learn about Guru Nanak from this story? Discuss this as a class and then write down the explanation a Sikh might give of this story saying what s/he learns from it.

● Imagine a new student joins your class who has no interests except religion and wishes only to pray, study religion and discuss religion and morality. How would you, your classmates and your teachers treat this new student? Give this student a name and write up a diary entry with your thoughts about her/him.

GURU NANAK'S ADULT LIFE

As Nanak grew to be a man, his father, Kalu, continued to try to turn him into a businessman. There is a story that Kalu gave Nanak twenty rupees and told him to go with a servant, Bala, to a nearby town and there buy something at the market that could be brought home and resold at a good profit. On the way, however, Nanak came upon a group of wandering Hindu holy men who had not eaten for several days. Nanak hurried to the town, spent all the money his father had given him on food, and returned to give the food to these men. Not surprisingly Kalu was not pleased with his son.

The messenger of Wahe-Guru

At the age of nineteen Nanak married. He went to work in the town of Sultanpur and there one morning he went to bathe in the river and mysteriously failed to return. He remained missing for three days and his friends and relatives searched for him with great anxiety. Then he reappeared as mysteriously as he had disappeared and his first statement on his return was: 'There is neither Hindu nor Muslim.'

Nanak later explained that during the three days he had been absent he had been in the presence of God and had been appointed God's messenger. During the rest of his life Nanak travelled widely teaching people and gaining followers. His message to them was that there is only one God, timeless and formless; this God – Wahe-Guru – does not make distinctions between people on the grounds of their race, sex or caste; all people equally can and should draw near to Wahe-Guru through the practice of Nam simaran.

Nanak made four great missionary journeys and it has been estimated that he walked a total of 12,000 miles. When he was about fifty, he settled with his family and followers in Kartapur and remained there until his death in 1539.

There are many stories of the adventures that Nanak had while travelling with his faithful companion Mardana, a Muslim musician, such as this one about a banquet given by the wicked Malik Bhago:

Nanak and Mardana arrived at a town called Saidpur and went straight to the carpenter's shop of a poor man named Lalo. After conversation Lalo invited them to stay with him. The only food he could offer was bread and boiled spinach but Nanak ate this with great pleasure. The next day Malik Bhago, the Hindu steward of the local Muslim chief, invited everyone in the village to a feast to show how wealthy he was. Nanak did not go and Malik was enraged. He sent for Nanak and

The blood of the oppressed was squeezed from the fine food on Malik Bhago's table

demanded to know why his sumptuous feast was being spurned while Nanak kept company with a poor, low-caste nobody like Lalo. Nanak took some bread he had brought from Lalo's house and held it in his right hand; he picked up some delicacies from Malik Bhago's table and held them in his left hand; squeezing the food in both hands milk was seen to drop from Lalo's bread, but from the food of Malik Bhago came drops of blood.

ASSIGNMENTS

- With a partner make up a conversation in which Kalu discusses his son Nanak with a merchant friend. Finish this by joining in the conversation yourself and giving your own opinion about the young Nanak.

- Retell the story of Lalo and Malik Bhago as a modern-day parable set in your home town. Give the characters different names and occupations. Finish the story by completing the sentence, 'This story shows us . . .'.

GURU NANAK'S SUCCESSORS

Guru Nanak had two sons, each of whom hoped to become the leader of the Sikh panth after the death of their father. However, both of them lacked the deep humility expected of a holy man. One story tells that when Guru Nanak dropped a water jug into a muddy ditch his sons thought it beneath their dignity to retrieve it. However, a disciple of the Guru named Lehna was happy to recover it, wash it,

and then offer Nanak pure water to drink out of it. This devotion led Nanak to appoint Lehna to succeed him as Guru. Lehna took the name Angad which means 'limb' (like an arm or a leg) because he saw his work as Guru being connected to Nanak's work as a limb is to a body.

The Ten Gurus

This is a list of the ten Gurus of the Sikh religion with their year of birth and years as Guru:

1	Guru Nanak	b. 1469	d. 1539
2	Guru Angad	b. 1504	*Guru 1539–52*
3	Guru Amar Das	b. 1479	*Guru 1552–74*
4	Guru Ram Das	b. 1534	*Guru 1574–81*
5	Guru Arjan	b. 1563	*Guru 1581–1606*
6	Guru Hargobind	b. 1595	*Guru 1606–44*
7	Guru Har Rai	b. 1630	*Guru 1644–61*
8	Guru Har Krishan	b. 1656	*Guru 1661–64*
9	Guru Tegh Bahadur	b. 1621	*Guru 1664–75*
10	Guru Gobind Rai (Singh)	b. 1666	*Guru 1675–1708*

Guru Angad was succeeded by Guru Amar Das, who was an elderly man when he ascended the **Gur Ghaddi** (Guru's seat). Guru Har Krishan was only a child and he died of smallpox having been Guru for only three years. Two of the Gurus, Arjan and Tegh Bahadur, were martyred by Muslim rulers. Guru Ram Das founded the city of Amritsar. His son Guru Arjan was responsible for building the Harimandir Sahib and for making a

There are no pictures of the Gurus drawn in their lifetimes. It is, however, traditional to draw them as if they were all of similar appearance

collection of hymns, the Adi Granth, that would later be expanded into the Guru Granth Sahib as we have it today. Guru Gobind Rai (who was renamed Gobind Singh) founded the Khalsa panth (see pages 34–5) and he announced that the Adi Granth would become the Sikhs' Guru after his death.

Sikhs believe that all of the Gurus were equally inspired and guided by God, the Sat-Guru. Non-Sikhs may write as if Guru Nanak was a peaceful mystic while Guru Gobind Singh was a soldier and an administrator, but to devout Sikhs the message of Sikhism was passed on throughout the ministry of all of the ten Sikh Gurus and now continues to be passed on whenever the words of the Guru Granth Sahib are read with understanding. From a Sikh point of view there are no fundamental differences between the teachings of any of the Sikh Gurus.

ASSIGNMENTS

● Look at the traditional picture of the ten Gurus together. You will notice that they are painted as if they were almost identical. Why do you think they are painted in this way?

● Research the life of one of the nine Gurus who followed Guru Nanak and compare it to Nanak's life and teachings. Explain, from a Sikh point of view, how they complement each other. Explain also how any differences between them could be misunderstood by a non-Sikh.

KEY WORDS

Gur Ghaddi

SIKH SCRIPTURES

You may remember from the description of the Guru-dwara on page 5, that at the front of the hall there sat a person who read from the **Guru Granth Sahib**, and fanned it. As the worshippers entered the Guru-dwara they prostrated themselves before the Guru Granth Sahib and offered it gifts. You will realise then that this is no mere book to Sikhs, it is the living Guru of the Sikh panth.

The Guru Granth Sahib is never put on the ground but always kept on cushions, and when not actually being read it is covered with a beautifully embroidered cloth called a 'rumala'. Sikhs do not turn their backs on the Guru Granth Sahib when they are close to it. At the beginning and end of each day a procession will carry it above head height to or from its overnight resting-place. The room where it rests is set out very like a bedroom. The Guru Granth Sahib is literally put to bed at night.

Sikh families will not keep a copy at home unless they have a special room they can put aside for it. They will instead have extracts from the Guru Granth Sahib and the Dasam Granth (see below) in a small book called the 'Nitnem', and even this will be kept wrapped and in a high, clean place when not in use. The Nitnem contains the hymns used daily for private worship.

The Sikhs' living Guru is accorded all the respect that would have been accorded the human Gurus in their lifetimes. Here it is taken to its overnight resting-place

What is the Guru Granth Sahib?

It is a book that is always 1,430 pages long, written in the Gurmukhi script. It contains hymns written by six of the ten Sikh Gurus, and some others written by Sikh, Hindu and Muslim holy men whose teachings were in line with Sikh beliefs and were respected by Guru Arjan who first put the book together. The book was extended by Guru Gobind Singh, who added hymns written by his father, Guru Tegh Bahadur. It was originally known as the **Adi Granth**. (*Adi* means 'first' or 'most important'; *Granth* means 'collection'.)

The particular importance of this book comes from the special position given to it by the tenth Guru, Gobind Singh. From the time of Guru Nanak the Sikhs had a human Guru to guide and teach them. But in 1708 Guru Gobind Singh made it quite clear that after his death the Adi Granth would become the spiritual Guru to guide the Sikhs in their belief and behaviour. It is therefore believed by Sikhs to be their living Guru, filled with the same 'jot' that inspired each of the human Gurus.

Other Sikh scriptures

Guru Gobind Singh wrote religious poetry which he did not include in the Guru Granth Sahib, but which is collected in another book known as the **Dasam Granth**. (*Dasam* means 'ten', so this is the book of the tenth Guru.) Some hymns from the Dasam Granth are included in the Sikh daily prayers.

When Guru Arjan first compiled the Adi Granth it was a Sikh named Bhai Gurdas who actually did the writing, and his handwritten copy of the Adi Granth is still in existence. Guru Arjan invited Bhai Gurdas to include some of his own hymns in the Adi Granth but Bhai Gurdas replied: 'How can the master and servant sit beside each other on the same couch?' However, at a later date, Guru Arjan said that the hymns of Bhai Gurdas provide the key to understanding the Adi Granth and therefore these writings are held in the greatest respect by Sikhs.

A fourth collection of hymns, this one by another early disciple of the Gurus, Bhai Nandlal, is also held to be sacred by Sikhs.

ASSIGNMENTS

● Look at the picture. Imagine you have been asked by a non-Sikh to explain what is going on in this picture and why. Write a brief explanation that you think will help her understand.

● A non-Sikh visits a Guru-dwara and mistakenly thinks that Sikhs worship a book. Produce a pamphlet, which you might like to illustrate, explaining the truth about the way the Guru Granth Sahib is treated by Sikhs.

KEY WORDS

Guru Granth Sahib
Adi Granth   Dasam Granth

THE TEACHINGS OF THE GURU GRANTH SAHIB

The poetry of the Guru Granth Sahib is difficult to translate into English. It loses a lot of its beauty and perhaps some of its meaning, but something of its message may be understood from quotations such as these. The first was written by Guru Nanak:

Let deeds be the soil, the seeding God's word; let truth be the water you daily apply. ‖ Let faith be the crop you grow in your field, for thus you will learn of both heaven and hell.

Refrain:
Do not imagine that words are sufficient to raise us to heaven or save us from hell. ‖ Seduced by possessions and sensuous pride we fritter our lives away....
Why gather wealth and the goods of this world when the pathway to death lies ahead?

[Siri Ragu 27, AG pp. 23–4]

The following verse was written by the low-caste Hindu Ravidas (see page 60):

A lowly cobbler lacking skill. ‖ Yet others bring their broken shoes.
I have no awl to pierce the holes; ‖ No

knife have I to cut a patch.
Though others patch yet they know pain; ‖ I lack their skill and yet know God.
Thus Ravidas repeats God's Name; ‖ And thus eludes Death's evil grasp.

[Sorath 7, AG p. 659]

This was written by the Muslim Sheik Farid:

Why leave your home, why roam the wild, why spike your feet on thorns? ‖ Why seek him in the jungle waste, the Lord who dwells within?...
I thought that I alone had pain, yet what should meet my gaze, ‖ When from my rooftop looking out I saw the world ablaze.

[Shalok Farid 19 and 81, pp. 1378, 1382]

● Read and discuss with a partner these extracts. Try to explain the message of each passage as clearly as you can. Notice any teaching that the passages have in common.

God, the Sat-Guru, speaks to Sikhs from the pages of the Guru Granth Sahib

Akhand path

Sometimes the Guru Granth Sahib is read from beginning to end, aloud, all in one go. This is called an **akhand path** and it takes forty-eight hours. Different people take turns to keep the reading going while others attend to listen for parts of it. Everyone concerned will try to be present at the beginning and at the end. An akhand path occurs before any Sikh religious festival or after an important family or community event like a birth or a death.

ASSIGNMENTS

● Write a short piece explaining what value an akhand path might have for a family as part of birth or death rites.

● When a Sikh has a difficulty she might open the holy book at random and begin to read. She will believe that the passage she reads will have been chosen by God to guide her in her difficulty. Imagine one of the passages above was read in this way; explain how it could help someone with its teaching.

KEY WORDS

akhand path

GURPURBS AND MELAS

In the Sikh religion there are two kinds of holy days: gurpurbs and melas. Before any holy day, akhand paths will take place in Guru-dwaras.

A **gurpurb** is a day that celebrates or commemorates an event in the life of one of the Sikh Gurus, such as his birth or death. The birthdays of Guru Nanak and Guru Gobind Singh and the martyrdoms of Guru Arjan and Guru Tegh Bahadur are commemorated by Sikhs everywhere, but other gurpurbs will be marked only at Guru-dwaras that have a special connection with the Guru concerned.

A **mela** is a fair – a sort of cross between a market and a carnival. Melas do not have to be religious but in the Sikh tradition three melas have particular significance: Baisakhi, **Holla Maholla** and **Diwali**. Baisakhi is so important to Sikhs that we shall come back to it at some length, but let us look now at the other two.

Holla Maholla

In the Hindu religion there is a very popular spring festival called Holi. Guru Gobind Singh wanted the Sikhs to stop celebrating Hindu festivals so in 1680 he commanded them to gather at Anandpur at Holi time for a new sort of celebration. As well as music and poetry readings the Guru organised archery, wrestling and other sports that prepared the Sikhs to be good soldiers. It is said that Holla Maholla means 'attack and counter-attack'.

Diwali

It has been said that Diwali is *the* Indian festival. It is celebrated throughout India by people of all religions and occurs each year in the autumn. The story Sikhs like to remember at Diwali concerns the sixth Guru, Hargobind. He was wrongly imprisoned in the Gwalior Fort by the officers of the Mogul Emperor Jehangir.

In the Gwalior Fort at the same time were fifty-two Hindu princes who had also been imprisoned wrongfully. When Emperor Jehangir personally examined the case of Guru Hargobind he ordered that he should be released. But Hargobind refused to accept his freedom while the Hindu princes remained in prison. The message came back from the Emperor that Guru Hargobind could take with him to freedom as many of the princes as could hold on to his cloak while he walked through the narrow passage that led out of the fort. Hargobind managed to have made and delivered a cloak which could be let down so that there was a flowing train extending several feet behind him.

This family are preparing to carry candles to all rooms of the house to celebrate Diwali

With the fifty-two Hindu princes holding on to the train of his cloak, Guru Hargobind led them to freedom.

This action clearly showed the Sikh Guru's concern for those treated unjustly irrespective of their religion, and since that time Guru Hargobind has been also known as 'Bandi Chhor' (liberator).

Since 1984 and Operation Bluestar (see page 56) Sikhs have found it difficult to celebrate Diwali with their previous enthusiasm. Bhaupinder Singh, a student from Nottingham, explained:

'It is as though a cloud has passed in front of the sun. We cannot forget easily that thousands of our Sikh brothers and sisters were murdered by the Indian government and so we cannot, for a while, celebrate at the time of a great Indian festival in the way we did before.'

ASSIGNMENTS

● Retell the story of Guru Hargobind from the point of view of one of the Hindu princes. You can invent a name and reason for your false imprisonment but be sure to say what you thought of the Guru before and after your liberation. It might help to find out something about Jehangir and the Mogul Empire – look in an encyclopedia.

● Diwali is the festival of lights, and light is a common symbol for good things, darkness for bad things. However, light and dark, day and night complement each other, so list all the positive things about darkness/night and all the negative things about light/day. You could create a collage of pictures based on your list.

KEY WORDS

gurpurb   mela   Holla Maholla   Diwali

BAISAKHI

Baisakh is the name of the month when crops are harvested in the Punjab. It overlaps the end of March and the beginning of April. Hindus in the Punjab have a new year celebration at this time. Guru Amar Das said that at **Baisakhi** Sikhs should gather together for the celebration apart from their Hindu neighbours. Sikhs

have their Baisakhi celebration on or about 13th April.

Baisakhi in history

Over the years there have been many things for Sikhs to commemorate at Baisakhi. An ancient tradition says that Guru Nanak was born at Baisakhi. It was at the Baisakhi gathering of 1699 that Guru Gobind Singh founded the Khalsa panth (see page 34) and this is the most important event remembered at Baisakhi. In 1919 at the Baisakhi Fair in Amritsar (at a place called Jallianwala Bagh) a British Army general named Dyer ordered his men to shoot at the gathered Sikhs to break up their meeting. Nearly 400 Sikhs, many of them women and children, were killed. This too is remembered at Baisakhi.

Celebrations at Baisakhi

A particular ceremony associated with Baisakhi and widely carried out in Great Britain involves the washing of the Nishan Sahib flag-pole with 'lassi' (yoghurt and water) and the replacing of the flag and the cloth which covers the pole (**cholla**) with a new one. You may wonder why they wash it in yoghurt rather than with soap and water, but yoghurt is believed to have special cleansing qualities and all

Having washed the flag-pole it must then be dried

products of the cow are regarded in India as being especially pure. There are Sikhs who regard this washing with yoghurt as an unacceptable part of the ceremony because it involves a Hindu belief (the purity of cows' produce) that is not an authentic part of Sikhism.

Baisakhi is also the time for the Guru-dwara committees to be elected and for initiation ceremonies to take place (see page 40). Children hope for new clothes and maybe other presents as well. Where there are large Sikh communities, like in Birmingham and Southall, there will be processions through the town with perhaps some Sikhs on horseback. In Nottingham the Sikh Community and Youth Service arranges for young Sikhs to learn to ride horses so that an old Sikh tradition can be maintained.

ASSIGNMENTS

● Look at the picture. Imagine you are present on this occasion and explain this ceremony and its meaning to a group of non-Sikhs who are with you.

● Imagine you were present when Guru Amar Das decided the Sikhs should gather separately from Hindus at important melas. In groups discuss advantages and disadvantages of doing this and why it might be helpful for Sikhs to have their own celebration. Write an account of your discussion and the main reasons why you think Guru Amar Das made this decision.

KEY WORDS

Baisakhi   cholla

BAISAKHI: THE KHALSA

Guru Gobind Rai realised that the Sikh community could very easily die out under Mogul persecution unless something was done. So on Baisakhi Day in 1699 he called all Sikhs together to a meeting in the town of Anandpur (City of Bliss).

The Guru stood in front of a tent. He began to talk to the Sikhs and said that he wanted someone to show his faith in the Guru by coming forward to have his head chopped off. No one came forward and some of the people there thought the Guru had gone mad and began to leave. But after the Guru had repeated the request three times he got a volunteer. The two men went into the tent and Gobind Rai came out again with blood dripping from his sword. He asked for another Sikh to prove his devotion to God and to the Sikh faith and someone else stepped forward. He too was taken into the tent. The crowd heard the swish of a sword cutting through the air and then the thud as it made contact. Again Gobind Rai came out with his sword dripping with blood. This was repeated three more times until five men had volunteered and had been taken into the tent. Then, to everyone's astonishment, Guru Gobind Rai came out of the tent with the five men. All were unharmed. These men were each given new saffron robes just like the Guru's.

The 'Five Beloved Ones'

Gobind Rai said that these five men were to be known as the **Panj Piaray** (the Five Beloved Ones) and they would be the first five members of a new family of Sikhs to be known as **Khalsa** (pure ones). All men who joined the Khalsa would add to their old names the new name of **Singh** which means 'lion'. Similarly women entering the Khalsa would all take the surname of **Kaur** which means 'princess'. Of the Panj Piaray one had been of the high Kshatriya (military) caste but the others were all of lower castes. From now on caste should be of no importance among the Sikhs.

Guru Gobind Rai initiated these five men using amrit. He took a steel bowl with water in it and began to stir the water with his khanda while he prayed. Then he accepted from his wife, Mata Sahib Kaur, an offering of sugar cakes which were dissolved in the water. This mixture, amrit, was drunk by each of the five men and also sprinkled on their eyes and their hair. Thus they became the first members of the Khalsa panth. The Guru then told them to initiate him into the Khalsa panth in the same way. The Guru changed his name from Gobind Rai to Gobind Singh. Afterwards other Sikhs present were initiated. They promised that in future they would always wear the panj kakke (five k's, see page 37) and keep the moral code of the Sikh religion.

ASSIGNMENTS

● Imagine you were a young Sikh present in Anandpur on Baisakhi Day 1699. Write a diary account of the day describing what you saw, what you heard and what you felt. Take a paragraph to sum up your thoughts at the end of the day.

● Some Sikhs believe that the Panj Piaray were actually beheaded and miraculously brought back to life. More cynical people suggest that goats were slaughtered in an elaborate charade. Does it matter? Think about this, discuss it and write up your conclusions.

KEY WORDS

Panj Piaray   Khalsa   Singh   Kaur

There are a number of ceremonies and functions within the Sikh religion which require the presence of five devout male Sikhs, who are given the title of 'Panj Piaray'. What do you think is happening in this picture and can you guess what the women are doing and why?

BAISAKHI: THE PANJ KAKKE

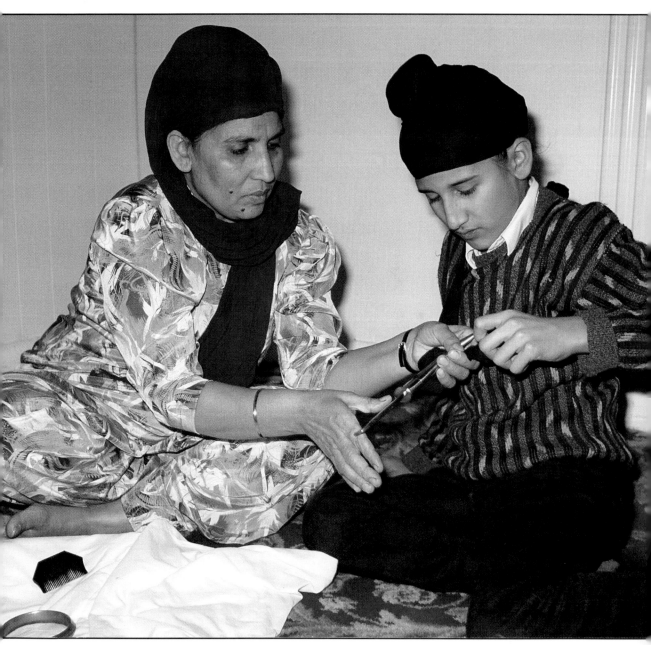

This woman is talking about the five k's to the boy. He is holding the kirpan; the kangha and kara can be seen lying on the kachh. Where is the fifth of the five k's?

During the time of Muslim persecution of Sikhs it was not unknown for a Hindu to be accused of being a Sikh and for him to be tortured and even killed for something of which he was innocent.

This problem was largely solved when Guru Gobind Singh encouraged his followers, men and women, to wear a distinctive uniform – the **panj kakke**, or five k's. (Those who have not been initiated may still wear them.)

What are the five k's?

Kesh Uncut hair. A Khalsa member must not cut or shave hair either on the head or anywhere on the body. The expression 'kesh-dhari' is sometimes used of a Sikh with uncut hair (see page 58). In India long hair is often the sign of a holy man.

Kangha A wooden comb. This is worn to keep the hair tidy and in place as well as to comb the hair. It symbolises cleanliness and discipline.

Kara A circular steel bracelet. The circle is an old symbol for God; it has no beginning and no end. Iqbal Singh, a twelve-year-old Sikh living in Nottingham, said:

> 'If ever I am tempted to do something bad I see my kara on my hand and it reminds me of my duty to Wahe-Guru.'

Daljit Singh, whom we met on page 18, says he likes to describe himself as being 'handcuffed to Wahe-Guru'.

Kirpan A sword with a curved blade. Sikhs are not pacifists; their religion teaches them that it is sometimes necessary to fight to defend the weak and oppressed and to obtain justice. English law allows Sikhs to carry the kirpan, although many Sikhs now carry just a small symbolic sword, sometimes on a key-ring.

Kachh/kachera White linen shorts. When worn by Sikh soldiers these short trousers allowed them a freedom of movement and speed which the Mogul armies did not have. They also symbolise chastity. Now they are usually worn like underpants, beneath trousers.

ASSIGNMENTS

● What other religious people in our society identify themselves by the way they dress? What advantages and disadvantages are there in wearing distinctive religious clothing in Britain today? Share your views with a partner.

● Imagine a discussion between two young Sikhs, one of whom observes the wearing of the five k's and the other of whom doesn't – what might they have to say to each other? Write the dialogue.

KEY WORDS

panj kakke   kesh   kangha   kara
kirpan   kachh/kachera

THE BABY-NAMING CEREMONY

When a baby is born into a Sikh family there is a special ceremony to be performed at the Guru-dwara at which the child will be given a name. The baby will be taken to the Guru-dwara by her/his parents and of course there will be other members of the family, and friends, present. This ceremony will normally occur during the main weekly meeting for keertan and so other members of the sangat will be present also.

Welcoming the baby

At the Guru-dwara amrit will be prepared while verses from the morning prayer by Guru Nanak (called the 'Japji') are read. (You will remember that amrit is a mixture of water and sugar crystals stirred with a khanda – a double-edged sword.) A kirpan is then dipped in the amrit and touched to the baby's tongue very carefully. The rest of the amrit is drunk by the mother.

Now comes the time when the baby's name is chosen. The Guru Granth Sahib is opened at random by the **granthi** who will read to the parents the first hymn on the left-hand page. The first letter of that hymn will be the first letter of the baby's name. The parents will now have a discussion about what name to choose; grandparents may well join in along with any brothers and sisters the baby has. Various names may be suggested before a decision is made and sometimes the parents will wish to go away and think for a few days before deciding on a name. The name chosen will be told to the granthi who will announce it to everyone present. He will add the name 'Singh' if it is a boy and the name 'Kaur' if it is a girl. Many Sikh names can be used for both boys and girls so sometimes in one class at a school there will be two pupils named, say, Ravinder, one a girl and the other a boy.

Maninder and then Iqbal explained how their parents chose their names:

'In my family mum and dad made a little dictionary of names before the ceremony so they could choose a name straight away whatever letter they got.'

'When the letter was announced they were stuck because not many Sikh names begin with 'I' and we already had an Inderjit and an Intipal in the family. That's why I was named after a Muslim friend of my dad's. But sometimes it's a bit of a problem – at school Muslim children sometimes ask me if I was a Muslim before I became a Sikh.'

It is very likely there will be a party at home to celebrate the name-giving and presents may be given to the parents and to the baby. The parents might thank God for their child by making a special donation to the Guru-dwara or to some other good cause.

ASSIGNMENTS

● Imagine you are a Sikh mother. Write a diary entry on the evening after your child's naming ceremony explaining what happened. Looking ahead confide your hopes and fears about the child's life.

● What different meanings might there be in touching the baby's tongue with sweetened water and a sword? Discuss this in class and write down the explanations you think are best.

KEY WORDS

granthi

People arriving at the Guru-dwara for keertan first queue to pay their respects to Guru Granth Sahib. The girl is making an offering. In the front row you will see the baby who is about to receive a name

TAKING AMRIT

The Sikh initiation ceremony is of special interest because some Sikhs never go through it, others do not go through it until they are quite old, and some go through it more than once.

Becoming amrit-dhari

For an initiation ceremony to take place it is necessary to have six Khalsa Sikhs and the candidate or candidates for initiation.

These people will commemorate the events of Baisakhi Day in 1699 when Guru Gobind Singh founded the Khalsa (see page 34). Five of the Khalsa Sikhs will take the part of the Panj Piaray and the other will serve as the granthi sitting behind the Guru Granth Sahib and reading the necessary passages. Another Sikh will stand guard at the door as only those participating may be present at this ceremony.

Those selected to be the Panj Piaray must make sure that each candidate understands what is involved in becoming

Khalsa and is suitable to undergo the ceremony. Amrit will be made as each one of the 'Panj Piaray' stirs the sugar into the water with a khanda while reciting the appropriate prayers from the Guru Granth Sahib. All eyes will be on the steel bowl in which the amrit is being prepared. The amrit is given to the candidates to drink; five times it is raised to the lips. Then it is sprinkled into their open eyes and over their heads. If any amrit remains it is given to the initiates to drink. Each drinks from the bowl and then passes it on.

An interesting aspect of the ceremony is that at times both those conducting the ceremony and the candidates adopt a position called **vir asan** with the right knee touching the ground and the left knee in the air. It shows humility like full kneeling would, but at the same time it makes it much easier to jump to your feet to defend yourself if attacked. It is a warrior's position. A person who has gone through an initiation ceremony and taken amrit becomes known as an **amrit-dhari** Sikh.

Hindpal Singh, whom we met on page 6, explained how taking amrit had changed his life:

> 'Beforehand I did sometimes drink alcohol and eat meat or eggs but not since I took amrit. And I have drawn away a bit from some of my non-Sikh or non-amrit-dhari friends.'

What is there in this picture that might lead you to think it is not a genuine initiation ceremony?

A Sikh student said he was preparing to take amrit and that for him the most difficult part was giving up eating meat – it had taken him four years.

Non-Khalsa Sikhs

Some Sikhs are not prepared to live according to the strict discipline of the Khalsa and they live their lives as what is called **sahaj-dhari** Sikhs. (Sahaj-dhari is often said to mean 'late developer'; see also page 58).

Others, especially living in places like England, delay their initiation until they are able to live according to the discipline as it can make life at college and work difficult. If Khalsa Sikhs lapse and disobey any of the rules they can ask to be initiated again and after doing some penance to prove their sincerity they will be initiated a second time.

ASSIGNMENTS

● Imagine you are the secretary of a Guru-dwara. Draft a letter to either a local headteacher or to the secretary of a sports or social club explaining the special needs of Khalsa Sikhs who belong to the organisation.

● The elements of the initiation ceremony: the steel bowl, the water, the sugar and the khanda each has a symbolic meaning. What do you think they are?

KEY WORDS

vir asan   amrit-dhari   sahaj-dhari

SIKH MARRIAGE

Marriage is very important. The Sikh religion believes that everyone should marry and that the relationship of a married couple should be like that of God and the true believer. The Guru Granth Sahib says:

When husband and wife sit side by side why should we treat them as two? ‖ Outwardly separate, their bodies distinct, yet inwardly joined as one.

[Guru Amar Das, Var Suhi 9:3, AG p. 788]

This idea that at the same time as a man and woman come together in marriage so both of them must be as a bride to God, is emphasised in many hymns from the Guru Granth Sahib which are sung during the Sikh wedding ceremony.

As the purpose of marriage is primarily spiritual, it is not surprising that the Rahit Maryada (code of conduct) discourages marriages between Sikhs and those of other religions. It says, ‘A Sikh’s daughter should marry a Sikh.’ However intermarriage between Sikhs and Hindus is common among some groups in India whilst in Britain there is a small but growing number of Sikhs marrying non-Sikhs.

● Do you agree or disagree that it is wrong for people of different religions to marry? What might be the effects of such marriages for the partners and the children?

The spiritual nature of Sikh marriage is very important to Tarnjit Kaur:

‘The only religiously important aspects of a Sikh wedding are that it should take place early in the morning and that it should take the form known as **anand karaj** [ceremony of bliss]. Hymns are sung and prayers are said before the Guru Granth Sahib. The couple indicate their consent by bowing together to the Guru Granth Sahib and what the couple are consenting to is that they will spend their lives in a spiritual journey, supporting each other in drawing ever nearer to Wahe-Guru and thereby ever nearer to each other. If in later life disagreements develop between husband and wife, they will be resolved by remembering: “Did we not bow together to Guru Sahibji?”’

● If God is related to the Sikh as a bridegroom is to a bride, what does this say about the relationship between a husband and wife? In what sense can a Sikh believe that the relationship between him/her and God may be like the relationship between a woman and her husband?

Finding a partner

Happy the girl, now awakened to love, when the matchmaker comes with his news.

[Guru Ram Das, Asa Chhant, AG p. 449]

This verse from the Guru Granth Sahib is evidence that in the early days of the Sikh religion it was usual for parents to use a matchmaker to find a suitable spouse for their daughter or son. The practice continues in an informal way in that friends may draw parents' attention to suitable partners for their offspring. However, Satpal Kaur Jandu, a Sikh student in London, insisted:

'Whenever people in England ask about Sikh marriage they always ask about arranged marriages, but there is nothing Sikh about this. It is common practice among all people in India, no matter what their religion is. It is already breaking down among Sikhs in England and in a couple of generations it will be gone. There are so many aspects to the traditional Sikh wedding which are just cultural, and a Westerner who became a Sikh could ignore them all.'

ASSIGNMENTS

● Take a non-Sikh religious wedding ceremony you are familiar with and think of the ways in which it is celebrated. What parts of it are religiously important? (If you are unfamiliar with any religious wedding ceremony, you can do the same exercise with a festival such as Christmas.)

KEY WORDS

anand karaj

A SIKH WEDDING

In the days leading up to a traditional Sikh wedding the bride will spend a lot of time with special female companions – probably sisters or cousins – while the rest of her family will be busy with the wedding preparations.

On the day before the wedding there is a ceremony known as the **milani**, when the groom's family visit the bride's family and gifts are exchanged. The wedding may take place in a Guru-dwara, in the bride's home, in a hired public hall or even in the open air, but the Guru Granth Sahib must be present.

The groom will sit in front of the Guru Granth Sahib and he will be joined there by the bride, who will sit on his left and traditionally be dressed in red (although some Sikh women now choose to wear saffron or blue). The groom has with him

What sort of conversation might the bride have with her bridesmaid before the wedding? What doubts and fears might she have?

an orange scarf, which will probably have been given to him by his mother, and during the service one end of it will be taken by the bride's father and put into her hand. There are special prayers to be said to bless the marriage and hymns to be sung. As we already know, the bride and groom show that they agree to the marriage by bowing to the Guru Granth Sahib, and then the groom leads his bride four times around the Guru Granth Sahib. Each of these circumambulations is known as a 'lav' (plural **lavan**), and a different verse from a hymn of Guru Ram Das is read before each of the four circumambulations and then sung as the couple go round.

After the wedding

There is of course much celebration after a wedding ceremony is over. Then comes the **doli**. Harbaksh Kaur Phull, a young Sikh teacher in Birmingham, explained:

'At the end of my wedding I returned without my husband to my parents' home. Then my husband came to collect me to take me to my new home. This ceremony is a time for goodbyes and it can be a particularly sad moment for the bride and for her parents, brothers and sisters. But these days things are not so bad because you know you can visit and make telephone calls.'

More wedding celebrations, this time at the groom's home, may carry on for a few days.

Sexual morality

Sikh men are taught to regard all women other than their wives as mothers, sisters or daughters. The Sikh religion has strict teachings against sexual relationships outside marriage. Divorce, although rare, is not unknown in the Sikh community. Divorcees may remarry using the same ceremony as at a first-time wedding. Widows and widowers are encouraged to remarry.

ASSIGNMENTS

● Do you think it is right to insist that marriage is appropriate for everyone? Write a script for a short radio discussion on marriage. Include among the participants a devout Sikh, a couple who are living together, a monk or nun (you may add others).

● Sikh wedding festivities often go on for a number of days. Is this a good or a bad thing from the point of view of.
a) the bride
b) the bridegroom
c) the two sets of parents?
List the advantages and disadvantages for each.

KEY WORDS

milani   lavan   doli

DEATH

Death is always sad. The friends and family of the dead person must learn to live without that person being with them any longer. Some members of the family may now have new responsibilities. A death also reminds everyone that each of us will die and so it is a time to think very seriously about one's own life.

Beliefs about life and death

Sikhs believe in the transmigration of souls. This is to say that a soul may have many births and deaths, both in animal and human form. A soul's transmigrations are, to some extent, governed by the law of **karma**, although God's grace can overrule karma. The law of karma teaches that all of a person's actions, both good and bad, have consequences, some of which will have effect during one's current lifetime and some in a future lifetime.

To be born a Sikh shows that a soul has come into this life with good karma. As a Sikh one has the opportunity of learning from the Sat-Guru (God) what is needed to escape from the cycle of births and deaths and to live eternally united to Wahe-Guru. But it is no part of Sikh belief that those of other religions may not also draw close to God and be united with God at death.

Their scriptures constantly remind Sikhs that this life is short and that they need to spend it in love and remembrance of Wahe-Guru.

> Each day that dawns must reach its end; ‖ All must depart, for none may stay. ‖ Our friends take leave, we too must go. ‖ Death is our fate, our journey far.
> *Refrain:* Heedless one, awake! awake! ‖ This life is transient doomed to end . . . . Life's end is near, its tasks undone, ‖ And darkness falls as night draws on. ‖ Let fools be warned by Ravidas: ‖ This mortal life must end in death.
>
> [From Suhi 2, AG pp. 793–41]

> All that we see must pass on and be gone from us, slipping away like shadows of clouds. ‖ Such is the world, a mere vision that perishes, leaving the Lord our sole refuge and friend.
>
> [From Gauri, AG p. 219]

The following passage, also by Guru Tegh Bahadur, overstates matters slightly to make a point:

> This world is unreal, a deceitful mirage; reflect on this truth in your heart. ‖ Sing praises to God for his gift of salvation; forever exalt his name.
>
> [From Devagandhari 2, AG p. 634]

Provide a caption to the picture, perhaps in the form of a poem, expressing your own feelings about death

It is not the Sikh belief that this world is unreal, after all, it was made by God. But the world is impermanent, it doesn't last, so it is a bad mistake for people to attach too much importance to material things. The only purpose of human life, according to Sikh belief, is for us to spend our time learning to love God and to draw close to God.

ASSIGNMENTS

● If you were told by a doctor that you would enjoy perfect health for the next six months and then die, how, if at all, would this change your life, behaviour and relationships? Write down your thoughts and then discuss the issue.

KEY WORDS

karma

A SIKH FUNERAL

It is important to realise that Sikhs believe that a dead person is beyond the help of the living. Therefore the rituals surrounding death are concerned with the decent disposal of a dead body and with the spiritual nourishment of the grieving family and friends. Although it is customary to cremate the deceased, this does not have any religious significance, and any other method of disposing of a dead body would be religiously acceptable.

A Sikh funeral traditionally took place on the day of death, and this is still the practice in tropical countries. In places like England, however, it is now more usual to delay for a few days to give all those who

Taking a body to the Guru-dwara before a funeral ceremony is becoming a custom among some British Sikhs

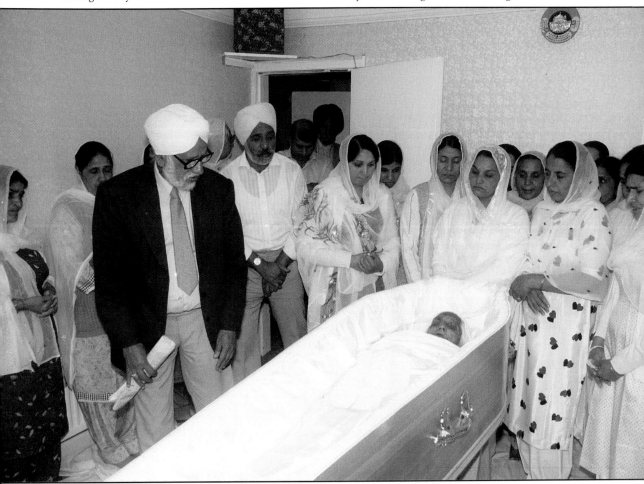

want to be at the funeral a chance to travel.

The body will be washed and dressed in the panj kakke. Among the hymns and prayers at the funeral service will be the evening prayer, Keertan **Sohila**. After cremation the ashes are scattered on water (a river, lake or sea), if this is possible.

The mourning family will often arrange for a copy of the Guru Granth Sahib to be installed in their home and it will be read aloud in its entirety over a period of seven to ten days (this reading is known as a **sidharan path**). During that time, friends and relatives will visit the family to pay their respects, join them in prayer and try to console them. Every visitor will be given karah parshad and langar prepared by the family.

Keertan Sohila

The Sohila is a quite difficult prayer (the word 'keertan' simply indicates that it is set to music), but it is worth looking closely at two short sections in translation:

> God has determined the time for my nuptials; come pour the oil at my door. ‖ Bless me, my friends, that I find that sweet union, dwelling as one with my Master and Lord.
> All must receive their last call from the Master; daily he summons those souls who must go. ‖ Hold in remembrance the Lord who will summon you; soon you will hear his command.

> Hear me friends, the time has come to all those who love the Lord. ‖ Thus we lodge that wealth with God which brings eternal peace.
> *Refrain:* Day and night our end draws nearer. ‖ Seek the guru; be prepared! Fear and evil rule the world, and only he who knows is saved. ‖ Only he whom God has wakened tastes the Name and knows the truth.
> Purchase that for which you come; the Guru's grace will lead you on. ‖ God will dwell within your heart and end the weary round.
> All-perceiving God who made us, grant this dearest wish I pray; ‖ Grant your slave the joy of serving all who praise the Name.

ASSIGNMENTS

● Read the quotations from the Sohila aloud, slowly, several times and in a group work out what you think they mean. Think carefully about these ideas and explain how Sikhs understand death. Then write about how this view of death compares with your own.

● In Britain, Sikhs are prevented from scattering human ashes on inland waters, so they send them out to sea or return them to India. Discuss whether this restriction is fair, and draft a petition giving reasons why the law should be changed.

KEY WORDS

Sohila   sidharan path

VALUES

MIRI AND PIRI, DEGH AND TEGH

Miri and piri

Do you remember the symbol on the Nishan Sahib? (See page 4.) It was a straight, double-edged sword (khanda), a chakkar (an ancient circular weapon) and two curved swords which are known as **miri** and **piri**.

The story is told that at the ceremony when Hargobind was installed as Guru, the man in charge of the ceremony made a mistake and put a sword on the wrong side of Hargobind's belt. He realised his mistake and was going to correct it when Hargobind said he should leave it and give him another sword for the other side of his belt.

'Miri' and 'piri' are related to two Arabic words: an *amir* was a military commander and a *pir* was a Muslim holy man; so miri and piri refer respectively to the strength and skills of the soldier and to the holiness and gentleness of the holy man.

Daljit Singh, a Sikh who lives in Nottingham, explained that for him miri and piri are linked to the Sikh ideal of the saint/soldier and to the inseparability of religion and politics:

'At the end of the day, if you've not got political freedom you've not got religious freedom . . . and politics without religion is barbarous.'

● Is it true that you can't have religious freedom without political freedom? In what sense is politics without religion barbarous? Can you relate this statement to a current situation, e.g. Northern Ireland, or the political role of Christian churches in, say, Central and South America, or of Islam in the Middle East and Africa? You could have a class debate on whether politics and religion should, or cannot, be kept separate.

Degh and tegh

A slightly different emphasis is given by the other pair of words often used to sum up Sikh values, **degh** and **tegh**. A 'degh' is a cooking pot, while 'tegh' is another word for sword. So a Sikh is someone who will feed the hungry and defend the oppressed. Daljit Singh explained:

'The degh represents the generous side of Sikhism, the Guru-ka-langar will go on for ever, and yet the tegh is there as well to defend freedom and help the oppressed.'

ASSIGNMENTS

● The Sikh woman in the picture is a volunteer at a hostel for the homeless and underprivileged in Southall. The hostel is maintained by a local Guru-dwara and the woman is helping people fill in some official forms. If you had an opportunity to put one question to this woman, what would it be? What do you think her answer might be?

● From what you know of the Sikh religion, write an explanation of why Sikhs believe military power and holiness, and the sword and the cooking pot, are important to them.

● Do you think that it is possible for holiness and military power to go together? Could someone be a good soldier and a holy person? Discuss this first in pairs and then as a class. Write up the main points of the class debate and also your own conclusions.

KEY WORDS

miri   piri   degh   tegh

SEWA

Try to think of an occasion when you found that serving someone else was helpful to you as well. Share your experience with a partner.

You may remember that in the section on Nam simaran (page 10) we learned that all of the Sikh religion could be summed up as bhakti (devotion to God) and that bhakti is demonstrated in two ways, through Nam simaran and **sewa** (pronounced *saiva*). Sewa is absolutely central to the Sikh religion.

Sewa means 'service'. Specifically, sewa is service for the benefit of others without any thoughts for oneself. The **Rahit Maryada** explains it like this:

> Sewa is an important part of Sikh life and the Guru-dwara is a school where community service may be learned, for example cleaning it, and carrying out repairs, fanning the congregation, looking after the shoes, giving water to drink and preparing or serving food in the langar.

You should not be surprised then, on visiting a Guru-dwara, to see a well-dressed and highly respected member of the Sikh community sweeping up or polishing other people's shoes. Do not forget that the second Guru proved his worthiness by his humble service (see page 24).

Sewa, selfless service offered to others, is an expression of devotion to Wahe-Guru

Helping others

Sewa also includes all charitable work, so visiting the sick or doing voluntary work for the community is important too. Sikhs have been famous for their charitable work right from the time of Guru Nanak and all Sikhs should give 'dass vanth' (one tenth of one's income) to charitable causes. The hospitals, orphanages and schools that have been set up by Sikhs have never been just for the benefit of the Sikh community but have been there for all who have needed them. Guru-dwaras in England have recently been collecting for the poor in Ethiopia and for children in Romania, while a Guru-dwara in Birmingham has committed itself to funding eye operations in the Punjab for both Sikhs and Hindus.

A Sikh student said that for him the best Sikh story about sewa concerns a man named Kanaiya:

'At the time of Guru Gobind Singh the Sikhs were fighting a battle and at the end of the day Bhai Kanaiyaji went on to the battlefield to give water to the wounded and to help them in any other way he could. Some of the Sikh soldiers were angry with him because he was helping the enemy soldiers as well as the Sikhs but he wouldn't stop. Sikhs grabbed him and took him to Guru Gobind Singh and complained about what he had been doing. Bhai Kanaiyaji said, "You have taught us to treat all people as children of God and to give sewa to everyone who needs it. I saw no enemies on the battlefield, only my brothers." The Guru said, "Well done, this is the kind of Sikh I wish to mint."'

ASSIGNMENTS

● Do you think the boy in the picture really benefits from what he is doing? Debate this in class and write down your reasons why you think he does or does not benefit.

● Imagine a young Sikh tells his mother or father he does not see the point of doing chores in the Guru-dwara. Write a dialogue between them in which the parent explains how sewa benefits the Sikh community and how it will help him in his life too.

KEY WORDS

sewa   Rahit Maryada

THE TURBAN

Sikhs have had all sorts of problems because of their **turbans**. At one time they could not get jobs that involved wearing a uniform because they could not wear caps, berets or helmets. Fortunately most uniformed organisations, like the police, now allow Sikh recruits to wear a turban of a suitable colour as part of the uniform.

A controversy of the 1970s concerned the wearing of crash-helmets on motor cycles. A new law said they had to be worn, but Sikhs said that they could not wear them. There were demonstrations, petitions and letters in the newspapers before the law was changed to say that a turban-wearing Sikh could ride a motor bike without wearing a crash-helmet. More recently Sikhs have had to battle for the right not to replace their turbans with safety helmets in some workplaces.

A boy said: 'There are still some teachers who call my turban a "towel" and threaten to pull it off.' So even in schools wearing a turban can be a problem.

Why is the turban so important to Sikhs and what is it exactly?

Rich, powerful and important

A turban is simply a length of cloth which is wound around the head and tied. At the time of the ten Sikh Gurus turbans were worn by rich, powerful and important men so first the Gurus and then their followers began to wear them to show that they were all rich, powerful and important (but not necessarily with worldly riches, power and importance). It is said that 'Every Sikh is a sardar' (sardar means chief) and Guru Gobind Singh maintained, as one Sikh put it:

> 'If you are going to live in this world live with dignity and pride, not like a mouse or a rat.'

Turbans can be of any colour but certain groups of Sikhs make a point of wearing a particular colour either as a fashion or to show that they support a particular group or party within the Sikh religion. Lengths of cloth to be made into turbans are a common gift among Sikhs.

The Rahit Maryada (which is binding on all believing Sikhs) states:

> Any clothing may be worn by a Sikh provided it includes kachera and, in the case of males, a turban.

You might wonder, if the turban is so important to Sikhs, why is it not one of the panj kakke? Well, at least one important twentieth-century Sikh teacher, Bhai Randir Singh, taught that wearing the turban was included with the requirement

For these Sikh construction workers, devotion to their Guru's command to wear the turban outweighs considerations of safety at work

for Sikhs not to cut their hair, and among Sikhs who agree with him women too wear the turban. (There are also some Western women converts to the Sikh religion who wear turbans.) However, the reason why Guru Gobind Singh did not include the wearing of the turban as one of the panj kakke is because he had already commanded Sikhs to wear it before the founding of the Khalsa panth.

When Sikh men play sport they will often cover their heads with a much smaller head-covering than a turban and this is called a keski. Boys normally wear a keski as small children and begin to wear the turban in adolescence.

ASSIGNMENTS

● You are a Sikh whose son has arrived home from school with a letter from the headteacher which says that all head-wear is forbidden in school and that if she makes an exception for your son the rest of the boys will want to wear hats too. Write her a letter explaining why you believe she is wrong and why you cannot compromise on this issue.

● Write an article on the Sikh turban for your local newspaper explaining what it means for a Sikh to say that his turban represents his riches, his power and his importance but not in a worldly way.

KEY WORDS

turban

A SIKH HOMELAND?

For fifty years at the beginning of the nineteenth century there was a Sikh state in the Punjab. It was ruled by Maharajah Ranjit Singh. After years of living under the oppression of the Mogul emperors it seemed a wonderful gift from God for Sikhs to be able to live under a wise and tolerant Sikh ruler. But the Sikhs' good fortune did not last. All too soon the Punjab became part of British-ruled India. The Sikhs fought bravely against the better-armed British troops but in the end they were defeated.

A Punjabi state

It is hardly surprising that when the Indian people began to campaign for independence from British rule Sikhs took a leading part. They believed that in an independent India there would be a Punjabi-speaking Sikh state. Hindu leaders of the home-rule campaign made such promises to the Sikhs. However, when in 1947 the British left India they separated the subcontinent into Muslim-ruled Pakistan and a secular state of India. The Sikh homeland was cut in two by the division. Because of hostility between Sikhs and Muslims nearly all the Sikhs migrated into the Indian Punjab or elsewhere in India.

Many Sikhs believe that from the beginning the Indian authorities have done everything in their power to prevent the Punjab being dominated by Sikhs or by the Punjabi language. Throughout India Sikhs believe they have been discriminated against and persecuted.

The land of the Khalsa

Many Sikhs now believe it is important for there to be a separate Sikh state in the Punjab to be called **Khalistan** – the land of the Khalsa. The campaign for an independent Khalistan has already been bloody. There have been many deaths, including that of a young Sikh leader, Sant Jarnail Singh Bhindranwale, and about 1,000 of his followers when Indian troops attacked the Harimandir Sahib in 1984 – the so-called 'Operation Bluestar'. That led on to the Indian Prime Minister, Mrs Indira Gandhi, being assassinated by two of her Sikh bodyguards who were later executed. The assassination resulted in riots in India and severe persecution of Sikhs, many of whom were murdered or badly beaten.

Sikhs, both in India and around the world, are still divided over whether there should be a completely independent Sikh state in the Punjab. The situation is not helped by the fact that many Hindus regard Sikhs as simply another group within Hinduism.

ASSIGNMENTS

● What is the Indian Government's attitude to the 'Sikh question'? In groups look back over the information on these two pages and do some further research, for example you could write to the Indian High Commission putting specific questions on the Government's policy over the Punjab and the Sikh religion.

● As a Sikh write a script for a local radio news item explaining the religious and cultural importance of a separate Sikh state.

KEY WORDS

Khalistan

The Punjab is a beautiful and fertile land

SIKHS WHO ARE DIFFERENT

Groups within the Sikh panth

We have already encountered the followers of Bhai Randir Singh, the Akand-Keertani Jatha (page 10). Other Sikh **sants** (another word for mahapurkhs) have followers who look to them for guidance and explanation. A group known as the Damdami Taksal are widely respected in many British Guru-dwaras for their knowledge and their piety. The Nihangs are a particular group of warrior Sikhs found still in the Punjab. All of these groups exist within the mainstream of Sikhi.

Western converts

There have been a number of Westerners who have found in the Sikh faith a religious path they could follow. In the USA a Sikh teacher of yoga named Harbhajan Singh Puri found many of his yoga students wanted to join their teacher's religion. These followers of Yogi Bhajan, as Harbhajan Singh Puri has come to be called, are known as members of the 3HO (Healthy, Happy, Holy Organisation). These American Sikhs are generally well thought of by the Sikh community, but it is important to emphasise that the yoga they practise is not a necessary part of the Sikh religion.

Non-amrit-dhari Sikhs

Having read this book it is possible that you may be confused. Perhaps in your class there is a Sikh with a short haircut, perhaps you know of a Sikh family that runs an off-licence or has alcohol in the home even though the men wear turbans, how can these things be? There are several possibilities.

Sahaj-dhari Sikhs: Even from the time of Guru Gobind Singh there were Sikhs who found the discipline of Khalsa membership too hard to take on. These people may say some of their daily prayers, attend the Guru-dwara sometimes and try to live according to the teachings of the Gurus to a certain extent. These people are known as sahaj-dhari Sikhs and it is always hoped by the community that one day such people will take amrit.

Many Sikhs who have not taken amrit may, however, be **kesh-dhari**, which means that they do not cut their hair and, if they are male, they wear a turban. Kesh-dhari Sikhs may wear other of the panj kakke but still permit themselves to do things forbidden to a Khalsa Sikh.

Patit Sikhs: Many Sikhs, when they came to Britain, believed they would have a better chance of finding work and accommodation if they shaved off their beards, cut their hair and ceased wearing the turban. Desperate to make a new life for themselves and their families, they

A Western convert helps in serving langar to visitors to the Guru-dwara

compromised their religious beliefs. If they had been Khalsa Sikhs they then became **patit** Sikhs. A patit Sikh is one who has gone through amrit but has, for whatever reason, broken one of the rules of Khalsa membership. It is always possible for a patit Sikh to repent and retake amrit, thereby again becoming Khalsa.

ASSIGNMENTS

● When a friend of yours talks about becoming a Sikh her parents are filled with horror. What might you say to her parents to help them understand the Sikh religion and what it will mean for their daughter to become a Sikh?

KEY WORDS

sant   kesh-dhari   patit

WOMEN IN THE SIKH RELIGION

> A woman, an untouchable and a drum – all made to be beaten.

This was written by Ravidas, a Hindu holy man living at the same time as Guru Nanak (some of Ravidas's hymns are included in the Adi Granth). The quotation reveals the attitude of many Hindus of the time to low-caste people and to women. Ravidas was himself low caste and so had direct experience of how such people were treated.

In the Hindu religion, ideas of purity and pollution are important. Women, because of menstruation and childbirth, are seen to be particularly dangerous sources of pollution. (The Hindu religion is by no means alone in having such beliefs, they are to be found in many of the world's religions.) However, Guru Nanak taught:

> Greed is the mind's pollution, falsehood pollutes the tongue; ‖ Eyes are polluted whenever they stray to another's wife or his worldly wealth. ‖ Ears are polluted by slanderous tales, by malice and wilful spite. ‖ He who was pure is enslaved by such sins and delivered in chains to hell. Foolish is he who believes in pollution.
>
> [From Asar Ki Var, AG pp. 462–75]

For this woman GP, both her years of study and her daily work are sewa

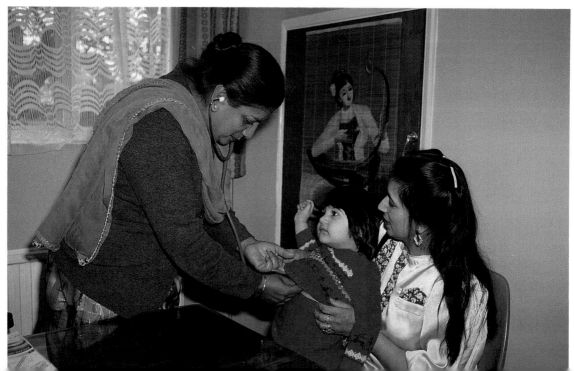

The importance of women

In the same way that the Sikh Gurus abolished caste differences among their followers, so they also abolished ideas of religious differences between the sexes. Guru Nanak wrote in one of his hymns:

From women born, shaped in the womb, to women betrothed and wed,|| We are bound to women by ties of affection; on women men's future depends. || If a woman dies we seek another, source of society's order and strength. || Why then should one speak evil of women, they who give birth to kings.

[From Asar Ki Var, AG pp. 462–75]

● Does this quotation suggest that Guru Nanak believed women and men are equal?

Many of the customs of the time concerning women were condemned by the Sikh Gurus. These included the killing of unwanted baby daughters, child marriage, the requirement for widows to commit suicide by throwing themselves on to the funeral pyres of their husbands, and the payment of dowries. It is also against the teaching of the Sikh religion for women to veil themselves.

When the Khalsa began, on Baisakhi Day 1699, Mata Sahib Kaur (the wife of Guru Gobind Singh) was one of those who helped to prepare the amrit. Women have led Sikh armies. But two Sikh students, Satpal Kaur Jandu and Tarnjit Kaur, spoke of how they saw the position of Sikh women today:

'The teaching of Sikhi [the Sikh religion] concerning women is great in principle, but over the years many Sikh men have been no better than other Indian men when it came to the treatment of women. It is very important that Sikh women come to understand their rights and duties.'

'You will hear Sikh men going on about "ijat" as if it was an important Sikh principle, just like they talk about every Sikh being a sardar [chief]. They would do better to remember the "five thieves of the soul" Sat-Guru has warned us of, anger, pride, jealousy, lust and attachment.'

(*Ijat* means 'honour' and it is often tied up, for a man, with the behaviour of the women in his family and his ability to control them.)

ASSIGNMENTS

● A recently published book says that any obstacles Sikh women face have nothing to do with the religion, but are the result of traditional Indian beliefs. From what you have now learned, would you agree that men and women are equal within the Sikh religion? Write a short piece giving your views.

Glossary and Index

independent Sikh state in the Punjab that many Sikhs aspire to *56*

Khalsa The company of the pure in heart – all Sikhs who have taken amrit and have not lapsed *34*

khanda A double-edged sword which is the centre piece of the Sikh symbol made up of the khanda, two kirpans and a chakkar. The whole symbol is also referred to as the khanda *5*

kirpan A sword with a curved blade – one of the five k's *37*

langar The Guru-dwara kitchen, the place where food is eaten at the Guru-dwara and the food itself – more properly 'Guru-ka-langar' *9*

lavan Lavan is plural. In the Sikh wedding service the bride and groom walk four times around the Guru Granth Sahib and this is known as lavan. Lavan is also used as the name for the four-verse hymn of Guru Ram Das used on this occasion and more properly known as the Suhi Chhant *45*

mahapurkh Literally 'great spirit' or 'superlative being'. A Sikh teacher respected for holiness and knowledge *10*

mela Fair *30*

milani A ceremony before a Sikh wedding *44*

miri Symbolically, the sword of worldly power *50*

Mool Mantra Guru Nanak's verses about the nature of God. It is the basic Sikh statement of belief in God *16–17*

Nam japna The repetition of God's names or verses from the scriptures *10*

Nam simaran Constantly remembering God's presence through meditation, prayer and the repetition of God's names or passages of scripture *10*

Nishan Sahib The flag that flies over Guru-dwaras – it is normally yellow, triangular and incorporates the khanda insignia *5*

pangat Sitting together to eat langar *9*

panj kakke The five k's *37*

Panj Piaray The 'five beloved ones' who were the first members of the Khalsa, also the five Sikhs chosen to officiate at Amrit ceremonies etc. *34*

panth The Sikh community as a whole *8*

patit A Sikh who has been initiated but who has lapsed *58–9*

piri Symbolically, the sword of spiritual power *50*

ragee A musician who accompanies devotional singing in a Guru-dwara *6*

Rahit Maryada A written code of conduct binding on all initiated Sikhs. There have been a number of these codes since the first was introduced by Guru Gobind Singh. The current one appeared in 1950 *52*

sahaj-dhari A 'late developer', a Sikh who has not yet been initiated *41*

sangat A Sikh congregation *7*

sant A Sikh respected for learning and holiness *58*

Sat-Guru God, the True Guru *17*

Sat-Nam God, the True Name *14*

sewa Service for the benefit of others *52–3*

shabad The hymns of the Sikh scriptures *10*

sidharan path A non-continuous reading of the Guru Granth Sahib *49*

Sikh A learner, a disciple or a follower *5*

Sikhi The word most used by Sikhs to describe their religion and its teachings *8*

Singh 'Lion', the name used by all male Khalsa members (and many other Sikhs and some non-Sikhs besides) *34*

So-dar Rahiras The evening prayer *14*

Sohila Hymns to be sung before going to sleep at night and also at funerals *49*

tabla Drums *6*

tegh Sword *50*

turban A length of cloth used by Sikhs as a head covering *54–5*

vir asan A half-kneeling position adopted by participants in the initiation ceremony *41*

Wahe-Guru 'Wonderful Guru' – the primary Sikh name for God *14*

yatra A visit to the Harimandir Sahib and other places associated with important events in the lives of the Gurus or the history of the Sikh religion *13*

Further reading

A useful address for information is the New Approach Mission for Occidental Sikhism, 52 Beaconsfield Road, Nottingham NG8 6FN (remember to enclose an SAE).

Arora, R. *Guru Nanak and the Sikh Gurus*, Wayland, 1987

Cole, W. Owen and Sambhi, P.S. *The Sikhs: Their Religious Beliefs and Practices*, Routledge and Kegan Paul, 1978 (*too difficult for most GCSE students but invaluable as a class/teacher resource*)

Cole, W. Owen and Sambhi, P.S. *A Popular Dictionary of Sikhism*, Curzon Press, 1990 (*invaluable as a class/teacher resource*)

Doabia, H.S. (ed.) *Sacred Nit-Nem* (Sikh Hymn Book), Mai Sewan, Amritsar: Singh Brothers, 4th edn. 1979

Duggal, K.S. *Sikh Gurus: Their Lives and Teachings*, The Himalayan International Institute of Yoga Science and Philosophy of the USA, 1987 (*a source of information on the lives of each of the Gurus*)

McLeod, W.H. (ed.) *Sikhism*. In *Textual Sources for the Study of Religion*, Manchester University Press, 1984 (*invaluable as a class/ teacher resource*)

Mansukhani, G.S. *et al. Learning the Sikh Way*, British Sikh Education Council, 1990

Singh, D. and Smith, A. *The Sikh World*. In *Religions of the World*, Macdonald, 1985 (*beautiful pictures, no activities*)

Singh, M. *Sikh Shrines in India*, Publications Division, Ministry of Information and Broadcasting, Government of India, 1975

Singh, R. and Singh, J. *Stories from the Sikh World*, Macdonald, 1987 (*aimed at a younger age group but can be enjoyed by all ages*)

Thompson, M.R. *Sikh Belief and Practice*, Edward Arnold, 1985 (*covers most of the GCSE syllabuses, found difficult by some students*)

LONGMAN GROUP UK LIMITED
Longman House, Burnt Mill, Harlow,
Essex CM20 2JE, England
and Associated Companies throughout the world.

First published 1993
Second impression 1994
ISBN 0 582 02966 X

Printed in Hong Kong
WP/02

Acknowledgements

We are grateful to the following for permission to reproduce copyright material:

The British Sikh Education Council for an extract from *Learning the Sikh Way* by Dr Gobind Singh Mansukhani et al (1990); Government of India, Publications Division, for an abridged and adapted extract from *Sikh Shrines in India* by Mehar Singh (1975); Guru Nanak Foundation UK for extracts from *Guru Granth Sahib*.

Additional sources:
W. Owen Cole and P.S. Sambhi, *The Sikhs: Their Religious Beliefs and Practices*, Routledge and Kegan Paul, pp. 6, 52, 54; W.H. McLeod (ed.), *Sikhism*, in *Textual Sources for the Study of Religion*, Manchester Univ. Press, p. 13; Harnam Singh Shan, 'Guru Nanak: His Life and Message', *The Sikh Courier*, Autumn 1984, Sikh Cultural Society of Great Britain, p. 20.

We are grateful to the following for permission to reproduce photographs:
© Mohamed Ansar, page **44**; © Cam Culbert, pages **7**, **11**, **16**, **23**, **24**, **29**, **30**, **36**, **51**, **52**; Chris Fairclough Colour Library, pages **12**, **32**, **40**; Judy Harrison/Format, pages **15**, **19**, **31**; Hutchison Library, page **4**; Magnum, page **57** (© Raghu-Rai); Christine Osborne, pages **8**, **21**, **39**, **48**; Picturepoint Ltd, page **47**; Tim Smith, pages **26**, **35**, **43**, **59**; John Twinning, page **55**.
Cover: Sikh wedding. Photo: © Cam Culbert

Picture research: Maureen Cowdroy

SIKHISM

General Editor: Clive Erricker

Themes in Religion is a series that presents a dynamic and human introduction to the six main world religions at GCSE level.

Each book is organised around the themes central to that religion, such as Beliefs, Scriptures and Worship. The final section in each book — Values — looks at how religions respond to the modern world.

Through straightforward text and a variety of tasks that encourage the student to look at their own ideas, and guide them from what they know already, the books give a progressive understanding of the main features and beliefs of each religion and an awareness of what it is like to hold such beliefs.

- emphasis on the diversity and living impact of each religion
- active learning approach
- stimulating photographs integral to the text
- careful selection of quotations from modern believers as well as scriptures
- wide variety of assignments which relate to GCSE syllabuses

This book explores the way Sikhs live out their faith in this country and across the world. Sikhs believe all people should be treated equally as children of the one God, regardless of gender, race or religion. The Sikh religion has teachings of great profundity and complexity, but its central beliefs, values and practices can be readily understood.

Other titles in the series:

Buddhism Lilian Weatherley
Christianity R. O. Hughes
Hinduism S. C. Mercier
Islam Alan Brine
Judaism Clive A. Lawton and Clive Erricker

THEMES IN
RELIGION

ISBN 0-582-02966-X

9 780582 029668